THE **MAKING** OF THE **UNITED STATES** FROM **THIRTEEN COLONIES**— THROUGH **PRIMARY SOURCES**

John Micklos, Jr.

Enslow Publishers, Inc.
40 Industrial Road
Box 398
Berkeley Heights, NJ 07922
USA
http://www.enslow.com

Original edition published as *From Thirteen Colonies to One Nation* in 2008.

Library of Congress Cataloging-in-Publication Data

Micklos, John.
  The making of the United States from thirteen colonies—through primary sources / [compiled by] John Micklos, Jr.
    p cm. — (The American Revolution Through Primary Sources)
  Rev. ed. of: From thirteen colonies to one nation.
  Includes bibliographical references and index.
  Summary: "Examines the formation of the United States during the American Revolution, including how the colonies came together to defeat Great Britain and the creation of the federal government and U.S. Constitution"—Provided by publisher.
  ISBN 978-0-7660-4133-2
  1. United States—History—Revolution, 1775–1783—Juvenile literature. 2. United States—History—Confederation, 1783–1789—Juvenile literature. 3. United States. Declaration of Independence—Juvenile literature. 4. United States. Constitution—Juvenile literature. 5. Constitutional history—United States—Juvenile literature. 6. Washington, George, 1732–1799—Juvenile literature. I. Micklos, John. From thirteen colonies to one nation. II. Title.
  E208.M454 2013
  973.3—dc23
                          2012022380
Future ditions:
Paperb .ck ISBN: 978-1-4644-0191-6   EPUB ISBN: 978-1-4645-1104-2
Single-User PDF ISBN: 978-1-4646-1104-9   Multi-User PDF ISBN: 978-0-7660-5733-3

Printed in the United States of America

To Our Readers: We have done our best to make sure all Internet Addresses in this book were active and appropriate when we went to press. However, the author and the publisher have no control over and assume no liability for the material available on those Internet sites or on other Web sites they may link to. Any comments or suggestions can be sent by email to comments@enslow.com or to the address on the back cover.

♻ Enslow Publishers, Inc., is committed to printing our books on recycled paper. The paper in every book contains 10% to 30% post-consumer waste (PCW). The cover board on the outside of each book contains 100% PCW. Our goal is to do our part to help young people and the environment too!

Illustration Credits: Collection of the Supreme Court of the United States, p. 31 (right); © Corel Corporation, p. 16; Domenick D'Andrea, courtesy of the National Guard, pp. 3, 14, 27; Enslow Publishers, Inc., p. 4 (bottom); The Granger Collection, NYC, pp. 22; © North Wind Picture Archives, p. 25; SuperStock/SuperStock p. 28; Independence National Historical Park, p. 31 (left); Library of Congress Prints and Photographs, pp. 1, 4 (top), 5, 9, 11, 12, 21, 33, 34; National Archives, pp. 17, 38.

Cover Illustration: Library of Congress Prints and Photographs (Painting by John Trumbull depicting the signing of the Declaration of Independence).

CONTENTS

1. **LEARNING TO WORK TOGETHER** 5

2. **BREAKING AWAY FROM BRITAIN** 14

3. **NOW WHAT?** 21

4. **CONSTITUTIONAL CONVENTION** 27

5. **A MORE PERFECT UNION** 33

   Timeline 42

   Chapter Notes 44

   Glossary 46

   Further Reading
   (Books and Internet Addresses) 47

   Index 48

LOOK FOR THIS SYMBOL **PRIMARY SOURCE** TO FIND THE PRIMARY SOURCES THROUGHOUT THIS BOOK.

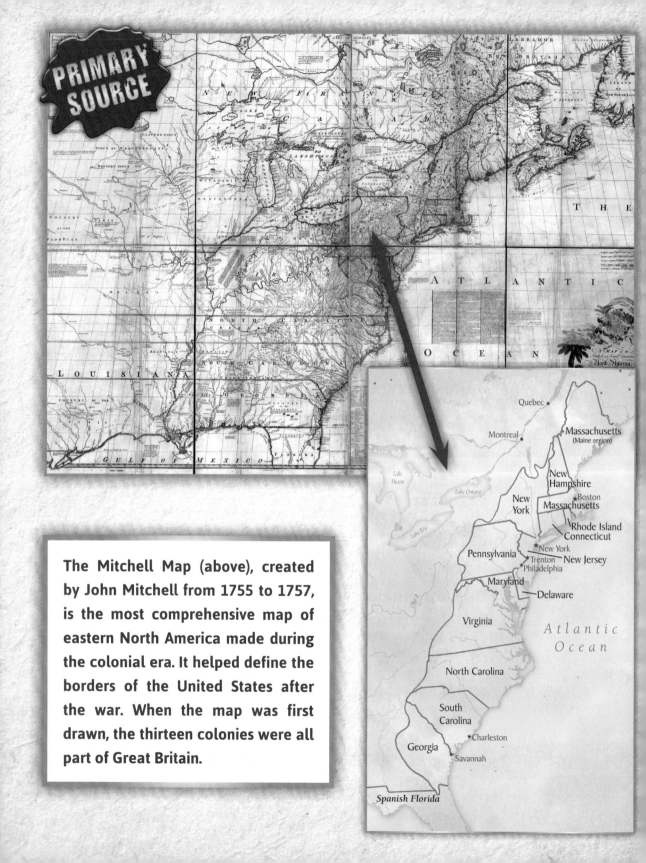

The Mitchell Map (above), created by John Mitchell from 1755 to 1757, is the most comprehensive map of eastern North America made during the colonial era. It helped define the borders of the United States after the war. When the map was first drawn, the thirteen colonies were all part of Great Britain.

CHAPTER 1

★

LEARNING TO WORK TOGETHER

By the mid-1700s, Great Britain had thirteen colonies along the eastern coast of North America. These thirteen colonies stretched from Massachusetts in the north to Georgia in the south.

In no way were the colonies united. Sometimes the colonies got along with one another. But sometimes they did not. For example, New York and New Hampshire clashed over which colony owned the land that would later become Vermont. Maryland and Virginia argued with Pennsylvania over Pennsylvania's borders.

For all their differences, the thirteen colonies had a lot in common. They were all part of the British Empire. People in the colonies were subjects of Great Britain's king. And they had the rights of British citizens.

The colonies all belonged to Britain. But each had its own colonial government. In most cases, this government was led by a royal governor. He was appointed by Britain's king. The governor, in turn, chose members of a council to advise him. But the colonies also established assemblies. These were legislatures, or groups, that dealt with the making of laws. Colonists elected the members, though typically only free men who owned property could vote. The oldest colonial assembly, Virginia's House of Burgesses, met for the first time in 1619.

The colonists believed that Britain's king was their rightful ruler. But over the years, they also came to believe they had the right to help decide how they were governed. In the 1760s, some colonists started to think this right was being ignored.

Parliament, England's legislature, had decided to make the colonists pay taxes on certain goods. In 1764, Parliament passed a law called the Sugar Act. It set a tax on sugar, molasses, and

Colonial Governments

Early in the history of the British colonies, royal governors held almost all the power. In most colonies, only the governor could propose a law. The assembly could only approve or disapprove it. Over the years, though, the colonial assemblies gained more power. By the early 1700s, they were allowed to suggest laws. They could also vote on how the colonial government taxed its people and how the government spent the money it collected. Gradually, the assemblies took on more and more responsibility for running the colonies. For the most part, British officials did not try to stop them.

other products imported, or brought into, the American colonies. The following year, Parliament passed the Stamp Act. This law required that colonists buy a tax stamp to put on all printed material, including books, newspapers, marriage licenses, legal documents, playing cards, and even dice.

These taxes were supposed to raise money to help the British government pay the costs of defending the American colonies. For instance, Britain had spent a lot of money sending troops to defend the colonies during the French and Indian War. Still, colonists believed the taxes were unfair. Colonists could not vote for members of Parliament. So they said Parliament should not have the power to tax them. "No taxation without representation" became a rallying cry for angry colonists.[1] Protests and riots broke out in several cities, starting with Boston. Groups calling themselves the Sons of Liberty threatened agents hired by the British to collect the stamp tax. Most of these officials quickly quit their posts.

The colonies had been used to acting alone. As a result of the Stamp Act, they began to work together. In October 1765, delegates (representatives) from nine of the thirteen colonies traveled to New York City for a gathering called the Stamp Act Congress. The delegates drafted a document in which they expressed their "warmest sentiments of affection and duty to His

Majesty's person and government."[2] But the delegates also said that colonists were entitled to all the rights and privileges of the king's subjects in England. One of those was the right not to be taxed unless they gave their consent, or permission. In England, this consent was given through elected representatives in Parliament.

This is a proof sheet of one-penny stamps made for the Stamp Act of 1765. This British law required the stamp to be placed on all printed materials in the thirteen colonies.

In the colonies, that consent had to be given through the elected colonial legislatures. So the delegates asked King George III and Parliament to cancel the Stamp Act.

Less than six months later, in March 1766, the British Parliament did end the Stamp Act. But the next year, it passed the Townshend Acts. These laws required colonists to pay taxes on imported glass, lead, paint, paper, and tea. In response, the colonies boycotted, or stopped buying and using, all English goods. Women in groups called the Daughters of Liberty began to spin and weave cloth so they did not have to buy fabric and clothing from England.

The colonists' boycott hurt the British economy. Eventually, Parliament canceled the import taxes on all goods except for tea. And the tax on tea was lowered. The British wanted to end the boycott. But they did not want to admit that Parliament had no right to tax the colonists. As King George said, "There must always be one tax to keep up the right."[3]

PRIMARY SOURCE

American colonists, especially those living in Boston, reacted to British taxes with protests, boycotts, and riots. This 1774 political cartoon depicts Bostonians harassing a British tax collector in an angry response to the king's taxes.

For some colonists, though, even one small tax was too much. In Philadelphia and New York, British ships carrying tea were not allowed to unload their cargo. In Boston, a group of angry colonists dumped 342 chests of British tea into the harbor on December 16, 1773. This became known as the Boston Tea Party.

The British responded harshly. In 1774, Parliament passed a series of laws to punish the people of Massachusetts and to get them to obey British authority. One law closed the port of Boston. Another took away most of the rights of the people in Massachusetts to govern themselves. Still, another forced colonists to

During the Boston Tea Party on December 16, 1773, a group of colonists dumped 342 chests of British tea into Boston harbor. This is the earliest known American depiction of the event made in 1789.

allow British soldiers to live in their homes—and this applied to all the colonies, not just Massachusetts. Colonists called the new laws the Intolerable Acts—meaning they considered the laws impossible to put up with.

In September and October of 1774, delegates from all the colonies except Georgia met in Philadelphia. The purpose of this meeting, known as the First Continental Congress, was to decide how to respond to the British.

The delegates had all been chosen by the legislatures of their colonies. Like the colonies they represented, they remained loyal to the king. They did not want to break away from England. But they believed Parliament had abused the colonists' rights. They wanted those rights restored. Until that happened, they made plans to set up a boycott on all trade with England.

The delegates sent their complaints to King George but not to Parliament. They hoped the king would act on their behalf. He did not. Relations between the colonies and the British government only worsened.

Then, on April 19, 1775, open fighting broke out. British soldiers and American colonists battled at the Massachusetts villages of Lexington and Concord. The American Revolution had begun.

CHAPTER 2

BREAKING AWAY FROM BRITAIN

On May 10, 1775, less than a month after Lexington and Concord, the Second Continental Congress met in Philadelphia. This time, delegates from all thirteen colonies were present.

In Massachusetts, the situation remained tense. Thousands of British soldiers were bottled up in Boston. Militias from Massachusetts and the other New England colonies had taken positions outside the city. The militias were ragtag groups. They were not professional soldiers. Instead, they were private citizens who trained together from time to time. They might fight in an emergency. But they could not be counted on to remain away from their homes for a long time.

The Continental Congress decided that a full-time army was needed to face the well-trained British troops. In June 1775, Congress created a regular army called the Continental Army. And Congress chose George Washington of Virginia as the army's commander-in-chief. But even at this point, most members of Congress believed they were fighting to protect their rights as British citizens. Very few of them wanted to break away from England. Few colonists wanted to break away, either.

In early July 1775, Congress drafted an appeal to King George III. It was called the Olive Branch Petition. In it, Congress said that the colonies remained loyal to the king. Their complaint was with the policies of his ministers and Parliament. Congress hoped that "the former harmony between [Great Britain] and these colonies may be restored."[1] The petition pleaded with the king to use his influence to resolve the conflict.

But George would not even receive the Olive Branch Petition. He declared the colonies to be in rebellion. He believed war was the only way to resolve the situation.

PRIMARY SOURCE

Congress selected a five-man committee to draft a document making the colonists' case for independence from Great Britain. Thomas Jefferson, shown here in this 1788 John Trumbull painting, wrote most of the document.

In early 1776, public opinion in the colonies began to shift. A writer named Thomas Paine suggested that the colonies should not try to settle their differences with the British. Rather, Paine said, they should break away once and for all. Although many people thought Paine was right, most colonists still did not favor independence.

The Continental Congress was also divided. On June 7, a delegate from Virginia introduced a motion (a formal proposal) calling for independence. "These United Colonies are, and of right ought to be, free and independent States," said Richard Henry Lee.[2] Congress debated Lee's motion for two days. The delegates could not agree. So they decided to put off a decision until July 1.

In the meantime, Congress formed a five-man committee to draft a document that made the case for independence. Thomas Jefferson of Virginia wrote most of the document, which became known as the Declaration of Independence.

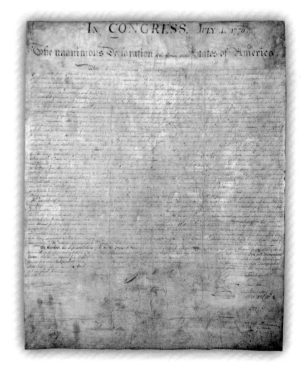

The Declaration of Independence said that the United States should be "totally dissolved" of all political connection to Great Britain. It also famously declared that "all men are created equal" and that they should have certain rights, including "Life, Liberty and the pursuit of Happiness."

No Equality for Slaves

It is one of the most famous passages in the Declaration of Independence: "We hold these Truths to be self-evident, that all Men are created equal."[3] Sadly, neither Thomas Jefferson nor the signers of the Declaration took this to mean that all would be treated equally. At the time, there were several hundred thousand black slaves in the thirteen colonies. Slavery would continue in the United States until the end of the Civil War in 1865.

Everyone, the Declaration stated, has certain basic rights. They include "Life, Liberty and the pursuit of Happiness."[4] Governments are set up—with the consent of the people—to ensure these rights. When a government resorts to tyranny, using its power wrongfully to take away people's rights, the people may change their government. The Declaration listed the many acts of tyranny committed by King George and Parliament.

Because of these abuses of power, the Declaration stated, the colonies owed no loyalty to the king, and "all political Connection between them and the State of Great-Britain, is and ought to be totally dissolved."[5]

On July 2, twelve colonies voted for independence. (New York's delegates did not vote because they had not been given approval to do so by their colonial legislature. New York voted for independence two weeks later.) On July 4, the Declaration of Independence was formally approved after Congress made some changes to it.

The colonies—which called themselves the "united States of America"—had cut all ties with the government of Great Britain.[6] But they had not yet created a new government.

It took until November 1777 for Congress to create a formal document of union for the states to approve. This constitution was called the Articles of Confederation. But it did not officially take effect until March 1781, when the last of the thirteen states accepted it.

In the meantime, Congress struggled to manage the war. Funding the Continental Army was a big problem. At the root of the problem was the fact that Congress had no power to tax the states. As a result, the Continental Army often did not have enough food, clothing, or weapons. Sometimes, the American soldiers did not get paid for long periods of time.

Still, with help from France, the Americans won a major victory in October 1781. A large British force surrendered to George Washington at Yorktown, Virginia. This marked the end of major fighting during the American Revolution.

The war officially ended on September 3, 1783. That day, representatives of the United States and Great Britain signed the Treaty of Paris.

The United States had won its independence. Now the question was whether the spirit of unity that brought the colonies together during the war would continue.

CHAPTER 3

★

NOW WHAT?

With the war over, a bright future for the United States seemed assured. But still the country faced major problems. For one thing, America had a huge war debt. Fighting the war had cost $170 million.[1] As of 1783, about $34 million remained to be paid.[2] It was unclear where the money would come from.

Under the Articles of Confederation, the central government remained weak. Congress had no authority over trade between the states. It had no power to tax. Therefore, it had no sure way of raising money.

PRIMARY SOURCE

No. 91]

THE State of New-Jersey is indebted unto *John Peck* of the County of *Essex* — in the Sum of *Thirty Pounds Six shillings & eight pence* — being for Militia Services; which said Sum shall be paid unto the said *John Peck* or his lawful Representative, in Specie, with Interest at the Rate of Six per Centum per Annum until paid. Witness my Hand this *Fifteenth* Day of *May* — One Thousand Seven Hundred and Eighty-*four*

C.   *Thos Clark* Commissioner.

After the war ended, the American economy crashed. The young nation could not pay its war debts, both at home and abroad. This is a bill of indebtedness for militia service issued by New Jersey to John Peck in May 1784. Peck was still owed money for his military service.

Congress did pass a measure to collect a 5 percent tax on imported goods. But all the states had to approve before such a measure became law. Pennsylvania and New York blocked it.

Other problems resulted from the weakness of the central government. For instance, pirates seized American merchant ships. There was no U.S. navy to protect these ships.

The states had worked together during the war. They knew they had to do so in order to survive. After the war, this changed.

Each state began pursuing its own interests, without considering the welfare of other states. Each state created its own trade rules. Some states set higher taxes on goods imported from other states than on goods imported from England.

Despite all this, most Americans did not want a strong central government. They had fought a long war to throw off British tyranny. They had no desire to see an American government take away their hard-won freedom.

By 1786, the economy hit bottom. The new nation could not pay its debts. It owed money at home to its own citizens and abroad to Spain, France, and the Netherlands. In fact, it could not even pay the charges, or interest, on its debts. Many Americans were suffering. In some areas, farmers who could not pay the taxes on their land lost their farms.

By August 1786, hundreds of farmers in western Massachusetts decided they had seen enough. Jails in the area were already filled with men who could not pay their debts. Others were facing a similar fate. Many of these farmers had served their country during the Revolution. Now, led by a former Continental Army captain named Daniel Shays, they took up arms once again. First Shays and his men forced courts in western Massachusetts to close. Then the angry mob of farmers began threatening to overthrow the state's government.

Hard Times for Farmers

In the years following the American Revolution, American farmers suffered when prices for their crops and other farm products dropped. The British were largely responsible. That is because Britain prevented American ships from trading in the West Indies. The American farm goods that would have been shipped there had to be sold at home instead. As a result, there were more products on the American market than there were people to use those farm products. And when the supply of a product is greater than the demand for that product, prices will fall.

Angry citizens in Massachusetts had seen enough men go to jail because they could not pay their debts. Led by Daniel Shays, a rebellion began. In this illustration, a Massachusetts blacksmith is served with a court order to seize his assets to pay for his debt during Shays Rebellion in 1786.

The governor of Massachusetts asked Congress for help. But because the Continental Army had been disbanded, there was no national army to put down Shays Rebellion. And Congress had no money to pay for troops to be recruited in Massachusetts. All it could do was ask the states to contribute money for this. Virginia was the only state that responded.

Eventually, wealthy citizens of Massachusetts donated enough money for a 4,400-man militia force. In February 1787, the main rebel group was finally defeated.

But news of the uprising—along with unrest in other states—was very troubling. George Washington feared that the new nation might be "approaching to some awful crisis."[3] Others shared this fear.

CHAPTER 4

⭐

CONSTITUTIONAL CONVENTION

In the wake of Shays Rebellion, many of America's leading citizens saw that the central government was not working well. Something had to be done to fix it. To discuss what, all the states except Rhode Island decided to send delegates to a meeting in Philadelphia. The meeting was scheduled to begin in May 1787. It became known as the Constitutional Convention.

Congress had given its approval to the convention. But it did not expect huge changes to come out of Philadelphia. Revising the Articles of Confederation to make the existing system work better was the "sole and express purpose" of the convention,

George Washington (at right on platform) speaks at the Constitutional Convention in 1787. Washington was selected as president of the convention.

Congress said. Most delegates to the Constitutional Convention shared that view.[1] However, a few delegates had a completely different idea.

On May 25, the Constitutional Convention officially opened. The delegates chose George Washington as president of the convention.

Four days later, after rules had been adopted, Washington called on Edmund Randolph to speak. Randolph, the governor of Virginia, presented a startling plan. It had been created by James Madison, another member of the Virginia delegation. Madison proposed a whole new system of government. It would be a federal system. This meant that the states would keep some powers of self-government, but in many areas they would yield authority to a federal, or national, government.

Power in the federal government would be divided among three separate branches. The legislative branch would be responsible for making laws. The executive branch would see that the laws made by the legislature were carried out. The judicial branch—the federal court system—would decide all court cases involving the government.

Madison's plan—known as the Virginia Plan—called for a two-house legislature. Members of the lower house would be elected directly by the people. This would be a big change. Under the Articles of Confederation, members of Congress were appointed by the state legislatures.

The newness of Madison's ideas took some delegates by surprise. Some grumbled that the Constitutional Convention should not even consider the Virginia Plan. But when Washington called for a vote, eleven states agreed to consider the plan. This practically guaranteed that the Articles of Confederation would be replaced.

However, trouble lay ahead. Madison created an uproar when he laid out a key element of the Virginia Plan. Under the Articles

Large and Small States

Large States: **Georgia, Massachusetts, North Carolina, Pennsylvania, South Carolina, and Virginia**

Small States: **Connecticut, Delaware, Maryland, New Hampshire, New Jersey, New York*, and Rhode Island****

*Sided with the small states

**Was not represented at the Constitutional Convention

James Madison (left) championed the Virginia Plan. This is a later portrait of him as President of the United States. William Paterson (right) developed the New Jersey Plan. This 1794 portrait shows Paterson after his appointment to the Supreme Court.

of Confederation, each state got one vote in Congress. Madison said that under the new system, the number of seats each state had in the national legislature would be based on the state's population. Large states liked this idea. They would get a greater voice in the government.

Small states, though, feared they would be bullied by the large states. On June 15, William Paterson of New Jersey presented an alternative to the Virginia Plan. The New Jersey Plan, as it came to be known, called for a one-house legislature. It also insisted that each state get only one vote in the legislature. Small states liked Paterson's proposal. However, the large states refused to even consider it.

Tempers flared. Neither side seemed willing to give in to the other's demands. By July 4, Luther Martin of Maryland said the Constitutional Convention was holding on "by the strength of a hair."[2] It appeared that the effort to create a new government might fail.

CHAPTER 5

★

A MORE PERFECT UNION

With the Constitutional Convention on the verge of collapse, Charles Cotesworth Pinckney of South Carolina made a suggestion. Each state, he said, should appoint one delegate to a "Grand Committee." The committee would try to find a compromise that large and small states could agree on.

Pennsylvania's delegate to the Grand Committee was Benjamin Franklin. He championed a solution that came to be called the Great Compromise. (It was also referred to as the Connecticut Compromise because parts had been suggested by Roger Sherman, one of Connecticut's delegates.)

PRIMARY SOURCE

Benjamin Franklin, shown in this 1778 portrait, helped create the Great Compromise that saved the Constitutional Convention. This compromise created a two-house legislature, combining elements of the Virginia Plan and the New Jersey Plan.

The Great Compromise kept a two-house legislature. Each state would get the same number of seats in the upper house (the Senate). This pleased the small states. The number of seats a state received in the lower house (the House of Representatives) would be determined by population. One seat per 30,000 people was the formula that was finally agreed on. Also, all pieces of legislation involving taxes and money had to come from the lower house. These measures pleased the large states. The Great Compromise passed, and the Constitutional Convention was saved.

The convention still had much work to do, however. One major issue was what type of leader would head the new government.

In the end, the delegates decided on an elected president. This was a new idea. In fact, it was revolutionary. At the time, governments throughout the world were headed by kings and queens. They ruled for life. When they died, power passed to their children. They claimed their power came from a God-given right—the "divine right of kings." By contrast, the head of the American government would be chosen by the people. The U.S. president would serve for a limited time, not for life.

Still, delegates to the Constitutional Convention wanted the chief executive of the United States to be powerful. The delegates worried that a legislature that was too strong might be a threat to liberty. It might try to take away the people's rights. A powerful president was needed, Gouverneur Morris of Pennsylvania said, to prevent this "legislative tyranny."[1] Of course, the president could not have too much power. Otherwise, he might become a dictator.

The Bill Of Rights

Some people worried that the new federal government would not protect individual rights. To help gain approval of the Constitution, the convention promised to spell out the rights all citizens had. James Madison authored twelve amendments to the Constitution. Ten were ratified. In 1791, they were officially added to the Constitution. Together, they are known as the Bill of Rights.

Some of the basic rights protected under the Bill of Rights are freedom of speech, religion, and the press; the right of people accused of a crime to have a speedy and public trial, at which they may confront witnesses against them; the right to a jury trial; and the right not to have one's property searched or seized unless the government can demonstrate a good reason.

The delegates saw that placing too much power in the hands of any individual or group could be dangerous. So they carefully created a system of "checks and balances." They divided power among the legislative, executive, and judicial branches of government. Over the years, the system of "checks and balances" would serve the United States well.

One issue the Constitutional Convention failed to resolve was slavery. In 1787, there were about 700,000 slaves in the country. Most of them lived in the South. Some delegates demanded that slavery be ended, but the Southern states did not agree. They depended on slave labor for many things. John Rutledge of South Carolina warned that people in the South would reject any plan that did not protect "the right to import slaves."[2] In the end, the delegates compromised again. They agreed that the slave trade would be allowed until at least 1808.

By early September, the essential parts of the Constitution were in place. Gouverneur Morris was tasked with refining the language of the document. He contributed a preamble, or introduction, that spelled out the reasons for creating the Constitution. "We the People of the United States," it said, "in Order to form a more perfect Union, establish Justice, insure domestic Tranquility, provide for the common defence, promote the general Welfare, and secure the Blessings of Liberty . . . do ordain and establish this Constitution for the United States of America."[3]

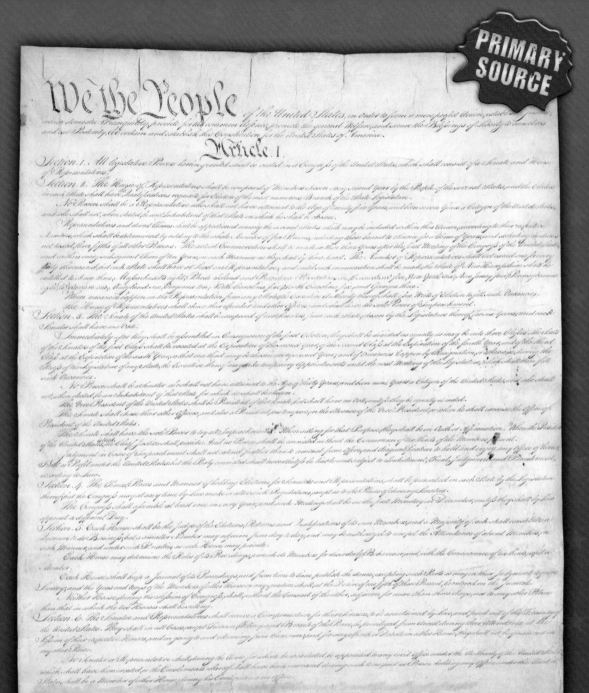

This is page one of the U.S. Constitution. The opening phrase of the preamble, "We the People of the United States," written by Gouverneur Morris, is clearly visible at the top.

The Electoral College

Delegates to the Constitutional Convention were divided on how the president should be chosen. Some wanted Congress to pick the chief executive. But this, it was feared, would give Congress too much control. Other delegates thought the president should be elected by a direct vote of the people. But such a method was considered difficult to manage in an era of slow communications. Plus, some delegates feared that candidates from big states would have too much of an advantage. And some delegates did not want to give too much power to the common people.

In the end, the convention approved an indirect method for selecting the president: the Electoral College. People in each state would vote for electors. The electors, in turn, would cast their ballots for president. The number of electors each state was assigned would be equal to the number of senators and representatives the state had in Congress.

On September 17, all twelve states represented at the convention voted to approve the Constitution. Only three of the forty-two delegates to the convention refused to sign the final document.

However, before the Constitution could go into effect, one more hurdle had to be overcome. Nine states needed to ratify, or formally approve, it. In some states, the debates were bitter. Supporters of the new Constitution were called Federalists. They wanted a strong federal (or national) government. Those who wanted more power to remain with the states were called Anti-Federalists.

On December 7, 1787, Delaware became the first state to ratify the Constitution. Pennsylvania and New Jersey soon followed. On June 21, 1788, New Hampshire became the ninth state to ratify the Constitution. That meant the Constitution was officially approved. In February of 1789, the first presidential election was held. The next month, the newly created U.S. Congress met for the first time.

Dates of Ratification

1787

Delaware: December 7

Pennsylvania: December 12

New Jersey: December 18

1788

Georgia: January 2

Connecticut: January 9

Massachusetts: February 6

Maryland: April 28

South Carolina: May 23

New Hampshire: June 21

Virginia: June 25

New York: July 26

1789

North Carolina: November 21

1790

Rhode Island: May 29

On April 6, the votes of the presidential electors were counted. George Washington was the winner. On April 30, 1789, he was sworn in as the first president of the United States of America. A new kind of government had come into being. A new and free country had been created.

TIMELINE

1764–1773

In 1764, Britain's Parliament passes the Sugar Act.

In 1765, Parliament passes the Stamp Act. In October, delegates from nine colonies meet at the Stamp Act Congress to decide how to respond.

In 1766, the Stamp Act is canceled.

The Townshend Acts are passed in 1767. Colonists boycott British goods.

On December 16, 1773, the Boston Tea Party occurs.

1774–1775

In 1774, Parliament passes laws designed to punish the people of Massachusetts. The colonists call these laws the Intolerable Acts.

In September and October of 1774, the First Continental Congress meets in Philadelphia.

On April 19, 1775, battles at Lexington and Concord mark the start of the American Revolution.

On May 10, 1775, the Second Continental Congress meets in Philadelphia.

1776

Thomas Paine publishes a pamphlet called *Common Sense*.

The Continental Congress issues the Declaration of Independence on July 4. This makes the break with England official but does not create a new government.

1777–1783

In November 1777, Congress creates the Articles of Confederation, a constitution for the union of the thirteen states.

In March 1781, the Articles of Confederation are officially approved.

On October 19, 1781, a large British force surrenders at Yorktown, Virginia.

On September 3, 1783, the Treaty of Paris is signed.

1786

The American government cannot pay its debts, and the nation's economy falters. Many farmers who are unable to pay their taxes lose their land. In Massachusetts, a former Continental Army captain named Daniel Shays leads a revolt of angry farmers.

1787

In February, a militia force paid for by wealthy Massachusetts residents puts down Shays's Rebellion.

On May 25, the Constitutional Convention officially opens in Philadelphia. Over the next four months, the delegates argue about the creation of a new form of government.

On September 17, the delegates vote to approve the United States Constitution. The document is then sent to the states for ratification.

On December 7, Delaware becomes the first state to ratify the Constitution.

1788

On June 21, New Hampshire becomes the ninth state to ratify the Constitution. This means that the Constitution has been approved.

By the end of 1788, only North Carolina and Rhode Island have yet to ratify the Constitution. North Carolina will do so in 1789; Rhode Island in 1790.

1789

In February, the first presidential election is held.

In March, the newly created U.S. Congress meets for the first time.

On April 6, the votes of the presidential electors are counted. George Washington is the winner.

On April 30, in New York City, Washington is sworn in as the first president of the United States.

CHAPTER NOTES

CHAPTER 1: LEARNING TO WORK TOGETHER

1. The phrase "No Taxation Without Representation!" was coined by Reverend Jonathan Mayhew in a sermon in Boston in 1750. By 1765, the term "no taxation without representation" was in use in Boston, but no one is sure who first used it. American colonial leader James Otis was most famously associated with the term, "taxation without representation is tyranny."

2. "The Declaration of Independence, July 4, 1776," *The Avalon Project at Yale Law School: Documents in Law, History, and Diplomacy,* 2008, <http://avalon.law.yale.edu/18th_century/declare.asp> (October 21, 2008).

3. John M. Thompson, *The Revolutionary War* (Washington, D.C.: National Geographic Society, 2004), p. 18.

CHAPTER 2: BREAKING AWAY FROM BRITAIN

1. "Journals of the Continental Congress, Petition to the King, July 8, 1775," *The Avalon Project at Yale Law School,* 2008, <http://www.yale.edu/lawweb/avalon/contcong/07-08-75.htm> (December 5, 2007).

2. Robert Middlekauff, *The Glorious Cause: The American Revolution, 1763–1789* (New York: Oxford University Press: 1982), p. 331.

3. Declaration of Independence.

4. Ibid.

5. Ibid.

6. Ibid.

CHAPTER 3: NOW WHAT?

1. Alan Axelrod, *The Complete Idiot's Guide to the American Revolution* (New York: Alpha Books/Penguin Group, 2000), p. 342.

2. Merrill Jensen, *The New Nation: A History of the United States During the Confederation 1781–1789* (Boston: Northeastern University Press, 1981), p. 382.

3. "George Washington, letter to Henry Knox, February 25, 1787," *The George Washington Papers at the Library of Congress, 1741–1799*, n.d., <http://memory.loc.gov/cgi-bin/query/r?ammem/mgw:@field(DOCID+@lit(gw290129))> (December 10, 2007).

CHAPTER 4: CONSTITUTIONAL CONVENTION

1. Thomas Fleming, *Liberty! The American Revolution* (New York: Viking, 1997), p. 356.
2. Ibid., p. 361.

CHAPTER 5: A MORE PERFECT UNION

1. Gouverneur Morris, quoted in William Howard Adams, *Gouverneur Morris: An Independent Life* (New Haven, Conn.: Yale University Press, 2003), p. 157.
2. Richard B. Morris, *The Forging of the Nation, 1781–1789* (New York: Harper & Row, 1987), p. 286.
3. United States Constitution.

GLOSSARY

boycott—To refuse to buy or use a product, often as a means of protest.

consent—Permission or agreement by a people to give authority to a government.

constitution—A document creating a government. The U.S. Constitution outlines the government's powers and lists some of the people's rights.

debt—Something owed; an obligation.

declaration—A formal statement. The Declaration of Independence announced America's break from England.

delegate—A representative to a meeting.

dictator—A person who rules with absolute power.

imported—Brought in from another country; often refers to goods brought in for sale.

interest—A charge for borrowed money, generally a percentage of the amount borrowed.

intolerable—Impossible to accept or bear.

jury—A body of impartial citizens who decide guilt and innocence in a courtroom.

legislature—A law-making body.

militia—Citizens who train as soldiers from time to time and are available to serve in an emergency.

Parliament—The legislative, or law-making, body of Great Britain.

petition—A formal request or appeal.

primary source—A document, text, or physical object which was written or created during the time under discussion.

ratify—To formally approve.

revolutionary—Bringing about a major or fundamental change.

tyranny—The unjust or cruel use of power.

FURTHER READING

Books

Anderson, Dale. *Forming a New American Government.* Milwaukee, Wis.: World Almanac Library, 2006.

Fleming, Thomas. *Everybody's Revolution: A New Look at the People Who Won America's Freedom.* New York: Scholastic Nonfiction, 2006.

Isaacs, Sally. *Understanding the U.S. Constitution.* New York: Crabtree Publishing, 2008.

Krensky, Stephen. *The Bill of Rights.* New York: Marshall Cavendish Benchmark, 2012.

Sonneborn, Liz. *The United States Constitution.* Mankato, Minn.: Heinemann-Raintree, 2012.

Internet Addresses

National Archives: Constitution of the United States
<http://www.archives.gov/exhibits/charters/constitution.html>

Library of Congress: Documents from the Continental Congress and the Constitutional Convention, 1774–1789
<http://memory.loc.gov/ammem/collections/continental/>

INDEX

A

Anti-Federalists, 40
Articles of Confederation, 19,
    21, 27, 29, 30

B

battles
    Lexington and Concord,
        13, 14
    Yorktown, 20
Boston, 8, 11, 12, 14
Boston Tea Party, 11–12

C

colonies, British
    government in, 5–13,
        14–16, 18–22
    See also Great Britain.
Congress (Articles of
    Confederation), 19, 21
Connecticut, 30, 33, 41
Connecticut Compromise.
    See Great Compromise.
Constitutional Convention
    (1787), 27–32
    and Electoral College, 39
    Grand Committee of, 33
    and slavery, 37
Continental Army, 15, 20,
    24, 26

D

Daughters of Liberty, 10
Declaration of Independence,
    17–19
Delaware, 30, 40, 41

F

Federalists, 40
First Continental
    Congress, 12
France, 20, 23

Franklin, Benjamin, 33
French and Indian War, 8

G

George III (king), 10, 13,
    15, 18
Georgia, 5, 12, 30, 41
Great Britain, 4–6, 15, 16,
    17–22
Great Compromise, 33–34

H

House of Burgesses, 6
House of Representatives, 34

I

Intolerable Acts, 12

J

Jefferson, Thomas, 16–18

L

Lee, Richard Henry, 17

M

Martin, Luther, 32
Maryland, 5, 30, 32, 41
Massachusetts, 5, 11–13, 14,
    23–26, 30, 41
Morris, Gouverneur, 35, 37

N

New England, 14
New Hampshire, 5, 30, 40, 41
New Jersey, 30, 32, 40, 41
New Jersey Plan, 32
New York, 5, 11, 19, 22, 30, 41
New York City, 8
North Carolina, 30, 41

P

Parliament, 6–11, 13, 15, 18
Paterson, William, 32
Pennsylvania, 5, 22, 30, 33,
    35, 40, 41

Philadelphia, 11, 12, 14, 27
Pinckney, Charles
    Cotesworth, 33

R

Rhode Island, 27, 30
Rutledge, John, 37

S

Second Continental
    Congress, 14
Senate, 34
Shays, Daniel, 24–26
Shays Rebellion, 24–27
Sherman, Roger, 33
slavery, 18, 37
Sons of Liberty, 8
South Carolina, 30, 33, 37, 41
Spain, 23
Stamp Act, 7–10
Stamp Act Congress, 8
Sugar Act, 6

T

Treaty of Paris, 20

U

United States Congress, 40
United States Constitution
    and Bill of Rights, 36
    preamble to, 37
    ratification of, 40, 41
United States of America, 19,
    37, 41

V

Vermont, 5
Virginia, 5, 6, 15, 16, 17, 20,
    26, 41
Virginia Plan, 29–32, 34

W

West Indies, 24